Even
Wounded Feet
Can Dance

A Path of
Loving Compassion

Teresa Zappia

Even
Wounded Feet
Can Dance

Authors note:

Born with a club foot, an early challenge that became the foundation of my life's journey toward healing and inner strength. Through lived experience, I have overcome physical challenges with resilience and a deep understanding of the powerful connection between mind and body.

By embracing myself with kindness, understanding acceptance and patience I built the inner strength to navigate life's challenges with grace. From this space of healing, and growth, I discovered the true ability to extend genuine compassion to myself and deep trust in life's unfolding.

These words have carried me through my darkest days, guiding me back to the light. May they now bring comfort and strength to someone who needs them too.

This book was written with love and intention. With every word I've written, I've felt guided and knowing you are here, eyes upon these lines reading them, fills me with gratitude and humble is the heart.

Thank you, truly.

With love,
Teresa

To Tony, Brendon, Megan and Ruby—

thank you
for your endless love and support.

Dear sacred watcher of my steps,

May we sit together, quietly—
not in battle, but in stillness. May
we turn toward the small, tender
girl you hold hidden in your arms.
Let us meet her with open hearts,
with soft eyes and gentler hands.
Let us listen— not to fix, not with
judgement but to understand, with
kindness, with compassion, with
love.

Imagine a moment where you meet
yourself—each part of you simply
meeting you, offering compassion.

Can we soften together?

Will you sit with me for
a minute? Just need to
know, I'm not alone.

Oh feet,
my faithful travellers,
you've borne the storm I
never knew—

*I'm so sorry that happen
to you.*

3

I invite you—
the silent visitor.
Called healing to
sit beside me.

You are not behind.
You are arriving,
at last, into your
own nurturing.

5

A tender clearing
opens wide enough
for truth to land
gently.

And where you're heading?
Trust that.

Trust yourself.

So, cradle your humanness
with open arms, and trust
that within your tenderness
lives a strength that does
not falter—

only deepens with
compassion.

Of course, you feel this way,
you were just a baby—

how were you supposed
to know.

My dearest heart,
I'm sorry for the times
I hurt you with my own
words—

you never
deserved that.

Oh love,
there's no voice to scold,
just open arms inside.

Sometimes the kindness
thing you can do is
meet yourself where
you are—

without fixing,
without scolding,
just listening.
You're remembering
that the softest landing
has always been in
your own care.

12

Begin with the understanding
that we all struggle, with
kindness nurture that, so
healing has room to grow.

Each act of kindness
toward yourself is a
seed of healing taking
root within you—

a gentle word, a
patient pause, a hand
resting over your heart,
in compassion.

It's okay to admit
things are hard.

There is a quiet
courage in admitting
when life feels heavy.
It's not a sign of defeat,
but a doorway to deeper—

honesty with yourself.

Soothe it over and over—

until it forgets how to
come back.

17

Meet the ache with gentle
hands, the way the ocean
meets the shore—

wave by wave, until peace
learns how to stay.

Today love,
what are you bringing to life
within yourself—

patience, hope, kindness, or
simply rest?

So choose with tenderness.
Choose with truth.
And in every act of care,
remember—

you are the one who decides
what nourishes your
becoming.

Oh love,
the only person who can
change you—

is you.

When you realise your
journey is ultimately your
journey.

Your inside.
Your outside.

You are allowed to—

speak to yourself
with the same
kindness you
offer others.

Wholeheartedly,
meet yourself there—

and see what happens.

Left. Right.
Feel your toes.
Feel your heels.
Feel that—

your needs are always met.

25

Your body knows the
earth's language—

it holds you, guides you,
every step rooted, steady,
sure.

Trust me when I say—

you are your
own number one
self-care priority.

When you honour
your wellbeing first,
life meets you with
more ease. Love begins
within you—

So let the world wait a
moment longer while
you tend to the quiet
corners of your soul.

Even though
that happened.

Be ever so tender
with those scars.

Even though the ache
once felt endless, look
at how you kept
walking—

one breath, one choice,
one quiet act of faith.
They've carried you
farther than you
know.

It happened, love—

forgive yourself.

You did the best you
could with the
understanding you
had then. You don't
need to carry the echoes
of what's already gone.

Forgiveness is how you
return home—

to the softness within you,
to the love that never left.

You got upset.
That's okay.

You're allowed to.

Your heart is simply
showing where it hurts,
reminding you that you
care deeply, that something
mattered enough to stir you.

Let the feeling breathe.
Let it pass through like
weather—

honoured, seen, and
free to go.

34

Give yourself the
biggest apology—

for what you didn't
deserve.

Now, let this be your quiet
turning point:

a moment to meet yourself
with tenderness, to honour
the strength that held you
upright when it was hard to
stand, and for the times you
didn't know how.

Let that apology be a
doorway to the peace
you've been waiting
for.

Oh love,
you can answer
with acceptance,
sometimes your softest
strength is simply saying—

"this too belongs."

You realise healing
isn't about erasing—

it's about allowing
what's here to rest
safely in your open
palms, and slowly,
grace gathers in the
spaces where
acceptance begins
to breathe.

Hold it up, let the
mirror rise—

softly honouring
the stories in your
eyes—the strength
behind your grace.

Let your reflection
remind you—

you've carried light
through shadows,
and still, you bloom,
a testament to how
love endures within you.

My love listen,
lasting change isn't
a destination—

it's a rhythm your body
learns to trust.

41

And then, my body
sighs in relief.

Once clenched
begins to sing.

Oh yes—
let your laugh echo.

No permission
slip required.

You're crazy!
You giggle like
a little girl.

You know you
get to lovingly
enjoy that.

The storm you're
facing, it's not the
end—

it's the ever so
tender repair.

So, I'm practicing
the art of pausing.
Of asking myself—

*"what do I truly
need right now?"*

Not today my darling.
We're not doing that
today.

Let's change it up.

Let's soften the story
we tell ourselves.
Let's let the feet rest,
feel the earth hum
beneath them. Each
step doesn't need a
destination, only a
whisper of kindness—

"thank you for carrying
me this far."

I know, it's a tough
moment—

you know you can
take a walk.

As your feet meet
the ground, let
nature—

hold what you no
longer need to
bear.

Each day, I get to
soften into myself—

to tend to old
wounds with
new love.

I no longer rush
my healing—

I meet it where it
stands, offering
patience instead of
proof.

Never ever doubt
your specialness—

you are not a maybe or
almost enough. You are
a quiet force tender and
tough.

Breathe into yourself,
let each inhale gather
all your courage, each
exhale release the
weight of expectation.
You are whole, exactly
as you are—

deserving of
your own care,
your own praise,
your own celebration.

She's here.
Sitting close,
wagging her tail,
ready to keep you
company—

together, we'll wait
until your heart feels
a little lighter.

55

Perhaps every
moment has
its purpose—

even the one's
wrapped in silence.

Guess what?
You chose to
feel different today.

Not better.
Not perfect.
Just softer.

Being softer isn't
weakness—

it's wisdom. It's the
moment you stop fighting
your feelings and start
listening to them. It's
where compassion begins
to grow, rooted in your
willingness to be kind to
the version of you who is
simply doing their best.

You did something brave—

you honoured your journey
by pausing mid-stride,
and that, my dear,
is how self-compassion
walks.

This is courage in its
truest form—

not in the running or
the reaching, but in
the tender act of
staying present with
yourself.

Step by step,
softly, bravely,
you are learning
that even stillness
moves you forward.

Even in stillness—

your faithful feet,
learning anew that
forward can also
mean standing gently
in your truth.

It's okay,
when you're not so
good. When your
smile feels forced,
and the day feels
too long—

it's okay.

So, rest dear heart,
feel what's real.

And know:
you're still worthy
when you're worn.

Oh love,
you don't have to.

You get to choose
what comes next.

Thank you, inner voice.

For always lifting me
when I forget my strength.

Trust me love,
you don't have to
bloom every day.

Some days just
breathing is a
miracle.

67

You are alive.
You are breathing.

That's no small thing.

But now, I'm seeing
that peace doesn't arrive
from the outside in.
It unfolds—

from the inside out.

I'm slowly learning that
life is better lived when I
begin tuning into what's
happening in here—

in my own heart,
my thoughts,
my feelings.

Teresa Zappia

I'm learning to love the
hush of release, the
whisper of goodbye—

to what no longer fits
the shape of my soul.

71

I'm learning that
letting go is not
loss, but a soft
return to what
was always mine—

the peace beneath
the noise, the stillness
that knows my name.

There's poetry in the way
I move, not in spite of my
feet—

but because of them.

But loving you is one
beautiful adventure—

a journey of rediscovery
through countless
moments.

But something sacred
happens when you soften
into your own rhythm—

when you stop apologising
for the way you were
made.

You're more than words
to me, a melody still
playing—

even when I forget
the song.

Wouldn't that be an
amazing gift—

to feel your arms
around you and
hear your tender,
nurturing, caring
voice.

Love doesn't always
have to arrive from
elsewhere—

sometimes, it's your
own soft voice, the
warmth of your arms
that reminds you—

*you were never
without care.*

Trust me when I say,

your story is acceptable.

Always.

Oh love,
hold this truth close:

in all its twists and
humble turns.

To my dearest,
thank you.

For always giving me
another chance.

Oh love,
I give you the soft
permission—

to feel,
to falter,
to begin again.

The teacher is here in
the mess, she came with
no need to be right.

Only understanding.

Thank you.
For your undivided
attention—

my presence
with myself is a gift
deeply appreciated.

Isn't it amazing… how
much you can change.

Not by force, but by
finally listening to the
quiet ache within.

The part of you
that's been whispering
all along,

"Please, be kind to me."

Teresa Zappia

I know my love,
you are shaped by the
truth of your inner being—

and that truth is tender,
wise and deeply enough.

So rest here a while.
Let your breath settle
back into you. You
don't need to prove
softness is strength—

it already is.

Seasons have passed.
Their lessons gathered—

like fallen leaves.

89

I bloom not from
perfection but from—

persistence.

My darling girl,
each step forward is a
celebration of your—

courage.

91

Right now,
holds everything
you need to begin—

honouring the
wisdom of
feeling.

Each step ahead
however small, holds
more promise than all
I've outgrown.

Soft winds of change
brush past my shoulders,
and I sway, not falling
but learning how to
dance with the weight
I've released.

I place my hand on the
place that aches most—
a soft gesture, a silent
vow:

I see you, I'm here.

Here, in this stillness,
your heart may rest—

letting kindness wash
over it, letting
compassion flow
like a peaceful river.

You lit a candle,
made some tea,
and found the quiet
part of yourself.

You walked,
you stretched,
you paused to
breathe.

As the water touches
my skin, I remind myself:

these feet are worthy of
care.

With each step,
the earth receives me.
The sand slips through
my toes, reminding me
that not everything must
be held so tightly—

some things are meant
to flow,
to shift,
to release.

You are listening to yourself always. So, let your voice be the first to say:

"you're doing just fine."

You don't have to earn
your place by always
being strong.

You are valuable—

just as you are
with your softness,
your stumbles,
your hopes and
your healing.

Oh honey,
even the way you sigh
when you stumble tells
the truth of you:

you are moving with a
tender, willing heart.

You choose yourself again,
and again,
and again.

And soon,
we will gently wave goodbye,
to what was never yours to
hold.
Because anything not born
from you was never meant
to stay.

And yes, I am learning
to bow to the beauty
of my feet.

To the parts of me still
healing—

"you're doing beautifully…
even now."

But the music— it forgives.

It slows with me, sways with
me, until I find my way back
in.

But the music— it bends.

It curves with my
uneven steps, fills
the quiet with gentle
echoes, and carries
me to the part of
me that always
stays.

Today,

how is your heart?
Whatever the answer—

let it be enough.

Notice the whispers of
feeling, the quiet shifts,
the sighs that rise and
fall—

all of it belongs to your
journey, all of it is exactly
what it needs to be.

Oh love,
your heart doesn't lie.

Your heart doesn't lie.

It whispers what
your soul already
knows and in its
quiet truth—

you will always find
your way home.

These feet have walked far—
through joy, through ache.
They, too, whisper for rest,
for gentleness, for care.

To pause and tend to them
is not selfish—

it is love.

113

Feel the quiet gratitude
rising from every step,
honouring the journey
they have carried—

in tending to them,
you tend to yourself,
guiding each step yet
to come.

Your past begins to feel
lighter, not because it
disappears, but because
you no longer carry it
with harshness, but with
compassion—

for who you were then.

Each day, I have the
freedom to begin from
within.

With love,
with kindness,
with acceptance.

Even when my steps
are tender, they are
still steps forward—

I honour my feet for
guiding me across
every terrain.

These feet tell a story of
resilience—

I will not judge them,
but thank them for
walking me through life.

These feet are my roots—

my strength,
my story.

119

And may love meet me
in every stride.

With each new day, I am offered the gift of giving myself the compassion I need.

With every sunrise, I am reminded to offer love to myself, and from that place let it flow outward.

Good girl.
You paused when the
dust rose, and whispered—

"it's okay" to yourself.

You're learning to sit with
all that you feel.

Just gentle truth in every
move.

Open the window my love,
let in light where doubt
once snoozed.

Let the light pour in,
a gentle tide washing
over old shadows,
and hear your own
voice whisper:

all is well, my love.

Softly.
Softening.
Softly—

it's never too late.

To bless the feet
that never faltered,
whispering thanks
to the soles—

that have kept you
moving through
it all.

128

With acceptance,
high heartedness,

life changes.

I wiggle my toes
and smile—

each step a little dance,
a tiny adventure,
a wink from the universe,
a footprint telling the story
of change.

Take up space.
Not to please,
not to prove,
be your tender,
your wild—

your unbeautiful truth.

Sit with your truth,
wild and open. Each
heartbeat is a living
reminder:

you belong here—

in all your messy,
radiant honesty.

My gift:
allowing myself
to be human—

to forgive my
missteps, soften
my edges, and
start again without
self-blame.

"I forgive you."

Say—

"I am learning",
"I have come far."

Say it again, until your
soul believes it, until
your heart stands taller.

I no longer linger in
the rooms of regret.
It is not the compass
I follow now.

I walk forward with
soft steps, cradling
the lessons, trusting
moments to guide me
towards—

what nourishes my soul.

Without even trying
without intention,
you are the one who
makes me smile and
you feel it.

You remind me that
connection isn't
always spoken,
sometimes it's
simply—

felt.

Buy the flowers—

not because you need
a reason but because
your heart whispered
"yes."

Because beauty is
meant to be brought
home.

Place them in a jar—

let the colours speak
joy into the corners
of your life.

Isn't it something how
shedding old skin reveals
not a stranger, but
someone you've
longed to meet.

You step forward,
and even your own
reflection smiles,
recognising at last
the friend you have
always held within
you.

And yes,
I am learning to
accept my beautiful
feet—

not as flaw,
but as blessing.

143

I was never broken—

only shaped by the hands
of mystery, carved by love
into a form uniquely mine.

No longer do I wish
you different,
for I know—

this is the way I am,
perfectly imperfect,
and wholly enough.

You've stumbled, yes,
and still you rise,
finding balance in
each new dawn.

You know it, don't you?
That your worth can't be
measured.

*I'm so deeply grateful
for who you are.*

Stay here a while.
Feel the pulse
of your life.

Each mark a memory,
each curve a testament
to grace.

You have held yourself
through storms,
and still, here you are—
whole, softly shining
enough.

You are already a gift,
already worthy,
already enough.

There is a kind voice,
soft, steady, and always
near, bearing words of
comfort and reassurance
you could never tire of
hearing.

It rests beside you,
patient and sure, a
hand on your shoulder,
reminding you that even
in the most still hours,

*you are fully held in
compassion.*

I would choose myself,
over and over—

for in every version of me,
love still whispers,

"I love you."

*From my heart to yours, thank you
for dancing beside me through
these words of compassion.
—Teresa Zappia
With love and gratitude*

Even Wounded Feet Can Dance